Reaching New Heights

Failure Is Not an Option – Quotes of the Day

By Photo Academy Italia

JEFF BEZOS
TOP INVESTMENTS

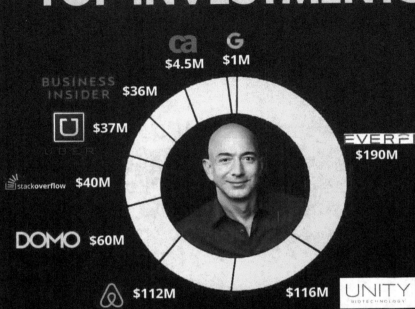

ca $4.5M **G** $1M

BUSINESS INSIDER $36M

U $37M

stackoverflow $40M

DOMO $60M

$112M

$116M

EVERFI $190M

UNITY BIOTECHNOLOGY

A doctor learns & understands medicine to earn money.

A lawyer learns & understands law to earn money.

A dietitian learns & understands nutrition to earn money.

A chef learns & understands culinary to earn money.

Yet, don't you think it's strange nobody learns & understands money?

CHANGE YOUR LIFE
IN ONE YEAR

REMOVE
NEGATIVE PEOPLE

COMMIT 100%
TO YOUR GOALS

STAY
HUMBLE

INVEST
IN YOURSELF

KEEP BUILDING
SUCCESS HABITS

LEARN FROM
MISTAKES

MONEY HACK:
THE RULE OF 7

BEFORE YOU SPEND MONEY, WANT 7 DAYS
BEFORE YOU MAKE THE PURCHASE TO SEE IF
YOU REALLY "NEED" IT. YOU'LL FIND THAT
YOU START BUYING LESS OF WHAT ISN'T
NEEDED.

RICH PEOPLE HOBBIES

INVESTING

KNOWLEDGE

GYM

DOING
BUSINESS

AVERAGE PEOPLE HOBBIES

PARTY

TV

GAMING

SHOPPING

THE MATH BEHIND SIDE HUSTLES

JOSH

Makes $40,000/year

Earns $200/week from his side hustle

First year : $50,400

Fifth year : $252,000

ALEX

Makes $40,000/year

Spends $200/week on going out

First year : $29,600

Fifth year : $148,000

THE POWER OF THE COMPOUND EFFECT

Watch what happens to a penny doubled every day, for thirty days.

DAY 1	$0.01	DAY 16	$327.68
DAY 2	$0.02	DAY 17	$655.36
DAY 3	$0.04	DAY 18	$1,310.72
DAY 4	$0.08	DAY 19	$2,621.44
DAY 5	$0.16	DAY 20	$5,242.88
DAY 6	$0.32	DAY 21	$10,485.76
DAY 7	$0.64	DAY 22	$20,971.52
DAY 8	$1.28	DAY 23	$41,943.04
DAY 9	$2.56	DAY 24	$83,886.08
DAY 10	$5.12	DAY 25	$167,772.16
DAY 11	$10.24	DAY 26	$335,544.32
DAY 12	$20.48	DAY 27	$671,088.64
DAY 13	$40.96	DAY 28	$1,342,177.28
DAY 14	$81.92	DAY 29	$2,684,353.56
DAY 15	$163.84	DAY 30	$5,368,709.12

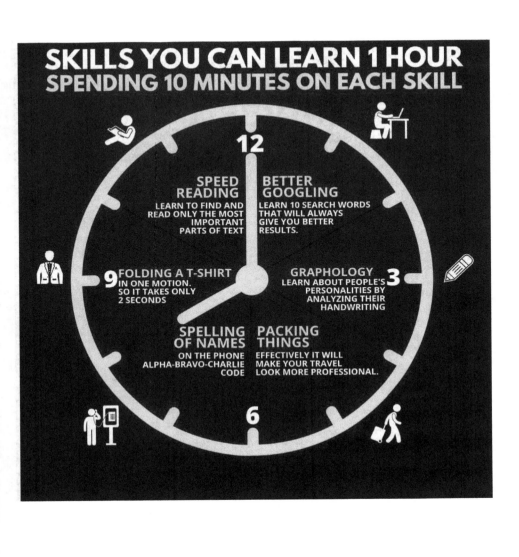

ADVICE TO
MY YOUNGER SELF

01. Read more.
02. Write more.
03. Practice public speaking.
04. Value friendship.
05. Memorizing is not learning.
06. Learn to invest.
07. You are not your job.
08. Know when to leave.
09. Find a mentor.
10. Trust your gut.
11. Slove your harder problems.
12. Networking is about giving.

HOW TO DECIDE FASTER

A MINDSET FOR MAKING FASTER DECISIONS

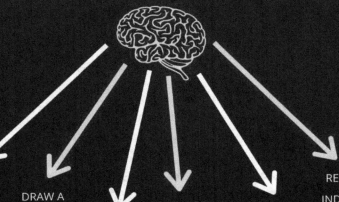

LIMIT YOUR OPTIONS

DRAW A HARD LINE BETWEEN GOOD AND BAD

LISTEN TO THE GUT FEELING

THINK OD YOUR TIME AS MONEY

KNOW THAT DECISIVESNESS GROWS WITH EACH DECISION

REMEMBER THAT INDECISSION KILLS

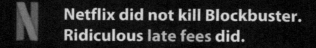 Netflix did not kill Blockbuster.
Ridiculous late fees did.

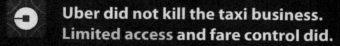 Uber did not kill the taxi business.
Limited access and fare control did.

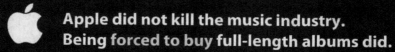 Apple did not kill the music industry.
Being forced to buy full-length albums did.

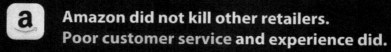 Amazon did not kill other retailers.
Poor customer service and experience did.

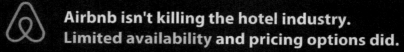 Airbnb isn't killing the hotel industry.
Limited availability and pricing options did.

**Technology by itself is not the disruptor.
Not being customer-centric is the
biggest threat to any business.**

HOW DO YOU USE THE INTERNET?

WASTES YOUR TIME AND MONEY:

| NETFLIX | GAMES | SOCIAL MEDIA | VIDEOS |

EDUCATES YOU ABOUT MONEY:

| COURSES | YT CHANNEL | BLOGS | PODCASTS |

MAKES YOU MORE MONEY:

| EBAY | AMAZON | CLICKFUNNELS | FIVERR |

EVERYDAY HABITS THAT DRAIN OUR ENERGY

TAKING THINGS
PERSONALLY

HOLDING ON THE
PAST

CHECKING FB
AND INSTA 24/7

OVERSTRESSING

SLEPPING IN LATE

FUELING DRAMA

HAVING A POOR
DIET

OVERTHINKING

POINTLESS SMALL TALK

THE MILLION DOLLAR
MORNING

5:00 AM		WAKE UP
5:30 AM		EXERCISE
6:00 AM		SHOWER
6:15 AM		MEDITATE
6:30 AM		READ
7:00 AM		BRAKEFAST
7:15 AM		WORK

AMOUNT OF MONEY YOU HAVE TO MAKE TO BE IN THE TOP 1%

IN DIFFERENT COUNTRIES AROUND THE WORLD

India: $77,000
Average annual income: $2,020

China: $107,000
Average annual income: $9,470

Italy: $169,000
Average annual income: $33,560

Brazil: $176,000
Average annual income: $9,140

South Africa: $188,000
Average annual income: $5,750

Canada: $201,000
Average annual income: $44,860

France: $221,000
Average annual income: $9,140

Australia: $246,000
Average annual income: $53,190

UK: $248,000
Average annual income: $41,330

Germany: $277,000
Average annual income: $47,450

Bahrain: $485,000
Average annual income: $47,436

USA: $488,000
Average annual income: $62,850

Singapore: $722,000
Average annual income: $58,770

UAE: $922,000
Average annual income: $40,880

THE PROCESS OF BUILDING A SUCCESSFUL BUSINESS

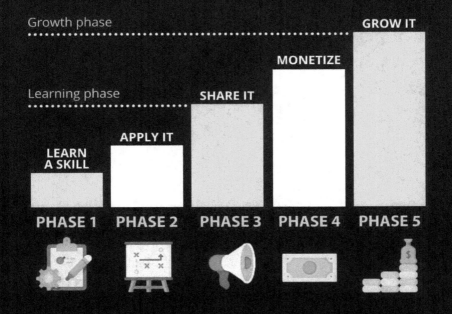

Growth phase

Learning phase

LEARN A SKILL

APPLY IT

SHARE IT

MONETIZE

GROW IT

PHASE 1

PHASE 2

PHASE 3

PHASE 4

PHASE 5

HOW TO CREATE A BILLIONAIRE

DON'T GIVE YOUR KID
$10 FOR DOING THEIR
CHORES. THIS WILL
RAISE YOUR KID WITH
AN EMPLOYEE MINDSET.

INSTEAD, REWARD YOUR
KID WITH $10 FOR EVERY
BOOK THEY READ. IT
WILL RAISE THEM WITH
A BILLIONAIRE MINDSET.

The best way to teach your kids about taxes is by eating 30% of their ice cream.

- BILL MURRAY

ONE - DAY RENT $700

PRICE : $60,000

86 DAYS RENT = $60,000

IMAGINE IF YOU HAD 10 EXCAVATORS.

YOU WOULD EARN $7,000 A DAY AND $2,10,000

A MONTH MINUS MAINTENANCE WORK

STAY AHEAD OF THE COMPETITION

✓	WATCH WEBINARS	WHILE THEY	WATCH NETFLIX	✗
✓	GO TO SEMINARS	WHILE THEY	GO TO CONCERTS	✗
✓	GO TO THE GYM	WHILE THEY	GO TO THE BARS	✗
✓	WORK ON YOUR SIDE HUSTLE	WHILE THEY	GO TO BED EARLY	✗
✓	DO WHAT YOU LOVE & TRAVEL THE WORLD	WHILE THEY	SLAVE AWAY AT THEIR 9-5 UNTIL AGE 65	✗

You can have a 9-5 AND have rental properties.

You can have a 9-5 AND have vending machines.

You can have a 9-5 AND invest in the stock market.

You can have a 9-5 AND wholesale real estate.

You can have a 9-5 AND be an entrepreneur!

ADVICE BY 21 SAVAGE

"I stopped wearing jewelry for a couple of reasons. One is because everybody wears jewelry. I outgrew it; I'm getting a little wiser and growing so... Another reason is because the richest people that I've ever met in my life, they've never had on jewelry."

MONEY IS EASY
ON THE INTERNET

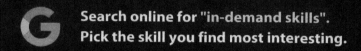 Search online for "in-demand skills".
Pick the skill you find most interesting.

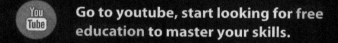 Go to youtube, start looking for free
education to master your skills.

Work for free to build a portfolio and sign
clients.
Then use your "free work" to advertise.

ONE DAY A YOUNG STUDENT ASKED HIS PROFESSOR
"WHAT'S THE DIFFERENCE BETWEEN SCHOOL AND LIFE?"

THE PROFESSOR REPLIED, "IN SCHOOL, YOU'RE TAUGHT A
LESSON AND THEN YOU'RE GIVEN A TEST. IN LIFE, YOU'RE
GIVEN A TEST THAT TEACHES YOU A LESSON."

YOU NEED 5 HOBBIES

ONE TO MAKE
YOU MONEY

ONE TO KEEP
YOU IN SHAPE

ONE TO KEEP
YOU CREATIVE

ONE TO BUILD
KNOWLEDGE

ONE TO EVOLVE
YOUR MINDSET

DIFFERENCE BETWEEN
RICH & POOR

Income

Debt

Poor People ← Continuous Debt Cycle →

Income

Liabilities

Saving

Middle Class ← 9-5 Liability Cycle →

Income

Saving

Investing

Profit

Rich People ← Asset Growth Cycle →

THINGS TO DISCUSS
WITH YOUR FRIENDS

**OPENING
BUSINESSES**

**INVESTMENTS
AND TRADES**

**GYM AND
DIET**

**SELF
DEVELOPMENT**

**ESCAPING
THE 9 TO 5**

**THE RIGHT
PARTNER**

You gotta step out of your comfort zone, Be broke for a while. Lose some friends. Have some sleepless nights. Most people don't get it through.

HABITS TO STOP RIGHT NOW

1) Living for the weekend
Work on your goals so you can build a life you don't need a vacation from.

2) Running out of money every month
It's time to start watching where every dollar goes and build more discipline for your financial goals.

3) Worrying what other people think
Stop being a prisoner to other people's opinions and letting that affect your life.

4) Not working on your goals after work
Being "too tired" after work is not an excuse. Don't just build someone else's dream at work, take action on your own.

TODAY'S SOCIETY

"How to buy index funds"

13 views

"Stock market basics"

54 views

"Billionaires morning routine"

47,083,203 views

If you're reading this, I DARE YOU to dedicate the next 6 months exclusively to your goals. No annoucments, just fall back & do the work!

EVERY TIME YOU

01. Stay out late
02. Sleep in
03. Party all weekend
04. Miss a workout
05. Overreact
06. Sit on the couch
07. Say you'll start tomorrow
08. Complain
09. Don't give 100%
10. Procrastinate

Your competition is winning.

Remember that.

CANCELLING PLANS TO READ IS OK

SKIPPING A PARTY FOR THE GYM IS OK

STAYING HOME TO COOK IS OK

LET'S ENCOURAGE IT AND RESPECT SELF IMPROVEMENT

THE 7PM - 2AM STRATEGY

IF YOU ARE WORKING A 9 TO 5 & THINK YOU DON'T HAVE TIME TO START SOMETHING ON YOUR OWN, LOOK AT WHAT YOU ARE DOING WITH THE SEVEN HOURS BETWEEN 7PM - 2AM. THIS IS THE TIME YOU NEED TO USE IF YOU WANT TO ACHIEVE MORE.

MONEYTUTORSHIP
@moneytutorship

It takes 21 days to form a habit?

No, it takes 30 days.

I read somewhere that it takes 90 days..

It can take more than 100 days!

Who cares?

Are you planning to stop?

the point of a habit is to do it every day.

So.. Keep doing it every day.

WEALTH IS THE POWER TO CHOOSE

FINANCIAL WEALTH - IS THE POWER TO CHOOSE HOW TO SPEND MONEY.

TIME WEALTH - IS THE POWER TO CHOOSE HOW TO SPEND YOUR DAY.

MENTAL WEALTH - IS THE POWER TO CHOOSE HOW TO SPEND YOUR ATTENTION.

65 WAYS YOU CAN MAKE $3000 FROM HOME

01. Executive VA	23. Baker	45. Shopify
02. General VA	24. Car Detailer	46. Sell T-Shirts
03. Marketing VA	25. Chef	47. Affiliate Marketing
04. Public Relations	26. Bike Messenger	48. Home Tutor
05. Community Manager	27. Dog Walker	49. Online Tutor
06. Social Media Manager	28. Pet Sitting	50. Music Lessons
07. Web Designer	29. Direct Sales	51. Online Teacher
08. Flier Services	30. Driver	52. Magazine Writer
09. Etsy Seller	31. Outbound Sales	53. Copywriter
10. Graphic Designer	32. Event Planner	54. Author
11. Photographer	33. Travel Agent	55. Bookkeeper
12. Videographer	34. Transcription	56. Proofreader
13. Music Composer	35. Podcast Editing	57. Project Manager
14. Stock Music Seller	36. Document Convert	58. Consultant
15. Voice Over Actor	37. User Testing	59. Yoga Instructor
16. Scrapbooking	38. Podcasting	60. Life Coach
17. Landscape Designer	39. Blogging	61. YouTuber
18. Homeschooler	40. Search Evaluator	62. Twitch Streamer
19. Courthouse Research	41. Coaching	63. Cooking Show
20. Errands Service	42. Online Selling	64. Product Reviewer
21. Order Fulfillment	43. Mystery Shopper	65. Exercise Instructor
22. Seamstress	44. Amazon FBA	

DISAPPEAR FOR
SIX MONTHS

 DON'T GO OUT TO PARTIES

 STUDY ALL DAY LONG, HIGH-PROFITABLE SKILLS (COPYWRITING, WEB DESIGN, DIRECT RESPONSE MARKETING ETC.)

 RECORD YOUR PROGRESS

 SELL YOUR SKILLS ONLINE

THOSE SIX MOTHS WILL CHANGE YOU LIFE FOREVER

THINGS THAT DISTRACT
YOU FROM BEING RICH

TOO MUCH NETFLIX

STAYING IN THE
COMFORT ZONE

WAITING FOR THE
RIGHT TIME

NOT ENOUGH
REST

OVER THINKING

PLAYING VIDEO
GAMES

15 IDEAS FOR PASSIVE INCOME

1) Start an ATM Business

2) Invest in Royalty Income

3) Start an Influencer Instagram Account

4) High Yield Savings Account

5) Sell on Amazon

6) Automate a Shopify Store

7) Grow one or multiple YouTube Channels

8) Create an Gaming App

9) Hold Growth Stock Long Term

10) Invest in Dividend Stocks

11) Invest in Rental Properties

12) Rent Out a Room

13) Buy a Vending Machine

14) Promote Other People's Products/Services as an Affiliate

15) Create a Product/Service and create an Affiliate System for it

12 HABITS THAT DRAIN YOUR WALLET

$5 Coffees

Bottled water

Lottery tickets

Eating out daily

Paid phone apps

Cigarettes

Credit card fees

Unnecessary uber's

Unused subscriptions

Not searching for discounts

Over priced cell phone

Spending money at the bar

RULES OF MONEY

1) Pay yourself first.

2) Learn how to invest.

3) Don't be a hater of it.

4) Give every dollar a job.

5) Spend less than you earn.

6) Have a plan and set goals.

7) Don't be a slave to money.

8) If you have it, don't flaunt it.

9) Keep your finances organized.

10) It's a game, learn how it works.

11) Always have an emergency fund.

12) Always make money work for you.

13) Learn how to make money passively.

14) Use it to solve problems in the world.

15) Know how to risk it and leverage it.

16) Don't use credit if you don't have cash.

17) It's not what you make, it's what you keep.

HOW TO HAVE
MORE TIME

01. Works in blocks.

02. Learn how to say no.

03. Cut down on TV/Netflix.

04. Plan your week in advance.

05. Limit your social media time.

06. Don't be busy just to be busy.

07. Don't do everything... delegate.

08. Unsubscribe from useless emails.

09. Don't be a perfectionist all the time.

10. Do most important tasks in the AM.

11. Be good at planning and organizing.

12. Disable notifications for useless apps.

13. Find tasks to eliminate or auomate.

14. One task to eliminate or automate.

15. Always set reminders on your phone.

16. Write stuff down so you don't forget.

ADVICE BY 21 SAVAGE

"I stopped wearing jewelry for a couple of reasons.
One is because everybody wears jewelry. I outgrew it;
I'm getting a little wiser and growing so... Another reason
is because the richest people that I've ever met in my life,
they've never had on jewelry."

BUSINESS IDEAS
WITH $0.00

1) Online event promoter
2) Scrapbookers
3) Online tech support
4) UX/UI designer
5) Bot marketer
6) Social media influencer
7) Social media manager
8) Freelance writer
9) E-Book author
10) Youtube personality
11) Podcaster
12) Custom illustrator
13) Errand service
14) Virtual assistent
15) Business consultant
16) Life coach
17) Graphic designer
18) Web designer
19) Personal trainer
20) Dance teacher
21) Music coach
22) T-Shirt designer
23) Auto detailer
24) Bookkeeper
25) Interior designer
26) Travel booking
27) Translator
28) Ghostwriter
29) Resume writer
30) Event planner

EVERYBODY IS
AN ADDICT

Some people are addicted to
junk food, watching TV, sleeping
in, social media,
and their bad habits in general
which give them temporary
happiness but never fulfillment.

Others are addicted to learning,
exercise, pushing themselves,
creating, planing and the high
they get from the achievement
and productivity which lead to
fulfillment.

THERE ARE 4 TYPES OF WEALTH:

 1) Financial wealth (money)

 2) Social wealth (status)

 3) Time wealth (freedom)

 4) Physical wealth (health)

Be wary of jobs that lure you in with 1 and 2, but rob you of 3 and 4

A FACT ABOUT MONEY

If you can't manage $1,000 then you can't manage $10,000.

You don't suddenly learn how to handle money by amassing more of it. This is why a lot of lottery winners lose it all.

Financial literacy is not a side effect of wealth. Wealth is a side effect of financial literacy.

HOW TO INVEST $1000

25%	25%	25%	25%
FOODS & BEVERAGES	PHARMA & HEALTH CARE	AI & ROBOTICS	IT SOFTWARE & SERVICES

• COCA-COLA	• NOVARTIS	• IBM	• APPLE
• PEPSICO	• PFIZER	• NVIDIA	• GOOGLE
• MCDONALDS	• ABBVIE	• HISILICON	• MICROSOFT
• STARBUCKS	• J&J	• INTEL	• FACEBOOK
• NESCAFE	• SANOFI	• ALIBABA	• AMAZON

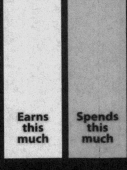

YOU MUST INCREASE YOUR INCOME

Canceling Netflix for $10/month
isn't going to help you.

Making your own coffee to
save $5 isn't going to help you.

Income must be increased!

Cutting back on basic garbage is fine but
don't pretend you're making progress.

Make more money,
spend it however you want.

GIVE YOURSELF 6 MONTHS

6 Months to be consistent at 1 thing.

- Hitting the gym
- Learning a new skill
- Creating/Selling a product
- Growing an audience

If you can stay consistent for
6 months, you're going to see
changes in your life.

That feeling is unsurpassed.

THE BIGGEST MONEY WASTERS

SMOKING

EXPENSIVE CLOTHES

BOTTLED WATER

GAMBLING

JEWELRY

EXPENSIVE CARS

FAST FOOD

10 THINGS TO QUIT RIGHT NOW

1) A sense of entitlement

2) Speaking poorly behind someone's back

3) Constantly complaining

4) Resentment

5) Making excuses

6) Worrying about the past

7) Interrupting people

8) Bragging about being busy

9) Fishing for compliments

10) Setting for mediocrity

SAVINGS: $30,000

INVESTMENTS: $150,000

CHECKING: $159.74

ME: "I'M BROKE"

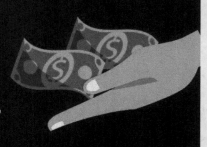

ONLY SOME WILL
UNDERSTAND...

THINGS YOU CAN CONTROL

YOUR
ATTITUDE

YOUR
NETWORK

YOUR
HABITS

YOUR
WORK RATE

YOUR
GRATITUDE

YOUR
PHYSIQUE

HOT INDUSTRIES TO INVEST IN

ROBOTICS

ELECTRIC CARS

BLOCKCHAIN

E-SPORTS

FINTECH

E-LEARNING

CANNABIS

BIG DATA

42 BUSINESS TO START FOR UNDER $2,000

- ONLINE RESEARCHER
- TOY MAKER
- ESSENTIAL OIL AND SOAP MAKER
- VINTAGE CLOTHING DEALER
- IMAGE CONSULTANT
- NON-MEDICAL HOME CARE
- MAKEUP ARTIST
- PERSONAL TRAINER
- FUNITURE REPAIR
- DECORATING SERVICE
- HANDY PERSON
- DIGITAL MARKETING
- SOCIAL MEDIA CONSULTANT
- SEO AND DIGITAL AD CONSULTANT
- RESUME SERIVCE
- MUSICA LESSIONS
- ARTS AND CRAFTS INSTRUTOR
- PET SITTING
- GARDEN CONSULTANT
- BACKYARD NURSERY
- BUSINESS PLAN SERVICE

- BIKE REPAIRS
- EVENT AND PARTY PLANNER
- WEDDING PLANNER
- JUMPING CASTLE RENTALS
- PET PHOTOGRAPHY
- GREEN BUSINESS CONSULTANT
- EXPENSE REDUCTION CONSULTANT
- CUSTOMER SERVICE TRAINER
- SALES TRAINER
- SMALL BUSINESS COACH
- FREELANCE PHOTOGRAPHY
- VIDEO PRODUCTION BUSINESS
- APARTMENT PREP SERVICE
- APP DEVELOPER
- MARKETING CONSULTANT
- AFFILIATE MARKETING
- EBAY SELLER
- WEB DEVELOPER
- WEBSITE FIPPER
- TRAVEL PLANNER
- LIFE COACHING

BEST DECISIONS TO MAKE IN YOUR 20S

1) **Understand you have** time

2) **Meet lots of people and** network

3) **Try new things and** hobbies

4) **Be patient and** don't stress

5) **Learn as much as you can**

6) **Build relevant skillsets**

7) **Get out of your comfort zone**

8) **Make continuous improvements**

9) **Learn about** yourself

10) **Discover what you're** good at

11) **Build good** habits and routines

12) **Fail fast, fail early, fail often**

13) **Don't let** opinions hold you back

14) **Put in the** work

15) **Manage your money well**

16) **Travel** as much as possible

17) **Define** success for yourself

18) **If you're working,** work to learn

19) **Indulge in** books

20) **Follow your mentors**

MOST PEOPLE

Has an idea

Thinks about it

Does absolutely nothing

THE 1%

 Thinks about it

Has an idea

Takes action immediately

HOW TO WIN THE DAY

- Plan your day the night before
- Wake up on time
- Avoid instant gratification
- Remove distractions
- Hold yourself accountable
- Focus & get to work

Focus on winning **each day**.
It will **add up**.

EASY WAY TO INCREASE WEALTH

BUFFETT SAYS " IF YOU CAN´T COMMUNICATE, IT'S LIKE WINKING AT GIRL IN THE DARK ... NOTHING HAPPENS. YOU CAN HAVE ALL THE BRAINPOWER IN THE WORLD, BUT YOU HAVE TO BE ABLE TO TRANSMIT IT".

3 TYPES OF INCOME

EARNED

STEADY INCOME YOU
GET FROM WORKING
A SALARY OR
COMMISSION JOB

INVESTMENT

LONG TERM PASSIVE
INCOME PRODUCED BY
OWNING ASSETS

BUSINESS

INCOME OR LOSS
EXPERIENCED FROM
TAKING RISKS AND
LEVERAGING MONEY

5 WAYS TO BOOST
YOUR INCOME

GET A SECOND JOB

FINDING A SECOND JOB IS
AN EFFECTIVE WAY TO
BRING EXTRA CASH IN YOUR
BANK ACCOUNT

AFFILIATE MARKETING

FIND A GOOD PRODUCT
AND START EARNING EXTRA
CASH BY REFERRING IT TO
WITHIN YOUR NETWORK

FREELANCE

SIGN UP TO PLATFORMS
LIKE UPWORK & FIVERR
AND START OFFERING
YOUR SERVICES

RENT OUT YOUR HOME

IF YOU OWN A SPACIOUS
HOME THINK ABOUT
RENTING A ROOM OR
BASEMENT WITH AIRBNB
OR CRAGISLIST

DRIVE PEOPLE AROUND

CHECK OUT PLATFORMS
LIKE UBER & LYFT AND
START MAKING MONEY
WHILE YOU DRIVE

WHAT SCHOOL TEACHES

What they teach:

- Photosynthesis

- Long division

- Trigonometry

- Shakespeare

- How to identify different dinosaurs

- Get permission to use the bathroom

What they should teach:

- Personal finance

- Nutrition

- Logic and reasoning

- How to think

- How to socialize

- Fitness & lifestyle

2 WAYS TO BECOME A MILLIONAIRE

1

FIND A **PROBLEM** AND SOLVE IT

2

FIND A **NEED** AND FILL IT

NO MORE EXCUSES

GET UP AT **5 AM** TO CATCH YOUR FLIGHT ON VACATION?

GET UP AT **5 AM** TO WORK FOR YOUR DREAMS?

NO PROBLEM!

IMPOSSIBLE!

THAT'S THE MINDSET WE HAVE TO CHANGE!

10 SIGNS YOU'RE DOING WELL IN LIFE

1) You have a roof over your head.
2) You ate today.
3) You have a good heart.
4) You wish good for others.
5) You have clean water.
6) Someone cares for you.
7) You strive to be better.
8) You have clean clothes.
9) You have a dream.
10) You're breathing.

BE THANKFUL FOR THE **LITTLE THINGS,**
FOR THEY **ARE THE MOST IMPORTANT.**

BEST SELF-DEVELOPMENT
BOOKS FOR 2020

**THE WAR OF ART
- STEVEN PRESSIFELD**

**THE 48 LAWS OF POWER
- ROBERT GREENE**

**THINK & GROW RICH
- NAPOLEON HILL**

**THE POWER OF
POSITIVE THINKING
- NORMAN VINCENT
PEALE**

**THE 7 HABITS OF HIGHLY
EFFECTIVE PEOPLE
- STREPHEM COVEY**

**HOW TO WIN FRIENDS
AND INFLUENCE PEOPLE
- DALE CARNEGIE**

THE BIGGEST LIES
ABOUT MONEY

"YOU'RE THROWING YOUR MONEY AWAY **ON RENT**"

"BUYING A HOME IS ALWAYS A **GOOD INVESTMENT**"

"YOU NEED A LOT OF MONEY TO **START INVESTING**"

"INVESTING IS COMPLICATED AND ONLY FOR **THE WEALTHY**"

"STUDENT LOANS ARE **GOOD DEBT**"

"YOU SHOULD ALWAYS AVOID **CREDIT CARDS**"

WHERE DOES IT HURT?

HEADACHE

STOMACH ACHE

PAYING COLLEGE
$40K/YEAR FOR
ACCESS TO FREE INFO
FOUND ON **GOOGLE**

RAISE YOUR STANDARDS

✓ SHOW UP 20 MINUTES EARLY FOR WORK

✓ GET RID OF THAT TOXIC REALTIONSHIP

✓ STOP EATING FAST FOOD

✓ READ MORE

✓ START EXERCISING

✓ FOLLOW THROUGH

✓ CREATE VALUE

✓ BE OF SERVICE

✓ DON'T ACCEPT BULLSHIT

BEING AN EMPLOYEE VS AN
ENTREPRENEUR

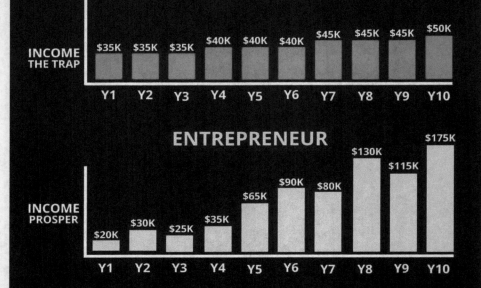

EMPLOYEE

INCOME
THE TRAP

Y1	Y2	Y3	Y4	Y5	Y6	Y7	Y8	Y9	Y10
$35K	$35K	$35K	$40K	$40K	$40K	$45K	$45K	$45K	$50K

ENTREPRENEUR

INCOME
PROSPER

Y1	Y2	Y3	Y4	Y5	Y6	Y7	Y8	Y9	Y10
$20K	$30K	$25K	$35K	$65K	$90K	$80K	$130K	$115K	$175K

STAGES OF YOUR MONEY JOURNEY

MAKE MONEY	SAVE MONEY	INVEST MONEY	MULTIPLY MONEY	MAINTAIN MONEY
1	2	3	4	5

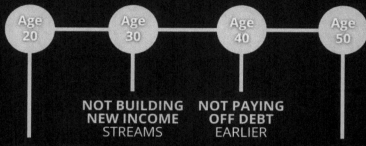

3 TYPES OF PEOPLE

DOCTOR   **ENGINEER**   **ENTREPRENEUR**

YOU SLEEP LIKE **YOU ARE RICH,**
I AM UP LIKE **I AM BROKE.**

8 INCOME STREAMS

1. **Earned Income** - Income from working job

2. **Profit Income** - Income from buying and selling

3. **Interest Income** - Income from lending money

4. **Royalty Income** - Income from others using your idea

5. **Dividend Income** - Income from owning stocks

6. **Rental Income** - Income from renting a property

7. **Capital Gains** - Assets increasing in value

8. **Residual Income** - Paid continuosly after work is done

INFLATION

Silently robbing your
purchasing power since 1913.

1913   **2020**   **2056**

YOUR 3 MONTHS LEVEL UP

 - **Wake up** early

 - **Cold** showers

 - **Read** 3 books

 - Brainstorm **Ideas**

 - Start your **side hustle**

 - **Invest** in yourself!

 - 30 min **exercise** daily

 - Eat **healthy** (No junk food)

 - Practice **gratitude**

 - Be **happy!**

Let's call it the PROTOCOL LEVEL UP

HOW TO BE A GOOD LEADER

 I was **wrong,** I am sorry

 I am **proud** of you

 What do you **think**?

 How can I **help**?

 I **trust** you

 Lead **by example**

TODAY'S SOCIETY

"HOW TO BUY INDEX FUNDS"
35 VIEWS

"HOW TO INVEST IN REAL ESTATE"
74 VIEWS

"HOW TO INVEST IN REAL ESTATE"
88 VIEWS

"BILLIONAIRES MORNING ROUTINE"
72,032,421 VIEWS

THE POWER OF THE COMPOUND EFFECT

Watch what happens to a penny **doubled every day,** for 30 days:

DAY 1	$0.01	DAY 16	$327.68
DAY 2	$0.02	DAY 17	$665.36
DAY 3	$0.04	DAY 18	$1,310.72
DAY 4	$0.08	DAY 19	$2,621.44
DAY 5	$0.16	DAY 20	$5,242.88
DAY 6	$0.32	DAY 21	$10,485.76
DAY 7	$0.64	DAY 22	$20,971.52
DAY 8	$1.28	DAY 23	$41,943.04
DAY 9	$2.64	DAY 24	$83,886.08
DAY 10	$5.12	DAY 25	$167,772.16
DAY 11	$10.24	DAY 26	$355,544.32
DAY 12	$20.48	DAY 27	$671,088.64
DAY 13	$40.96	DAY 28	$1,342,177.18
DAY 14	$81.92	DAY 29	$2,664,353,56
DAY 15	$163.84	DAY 30	$5,368,709.12

9 MISTAKES THAT KILL STARTUPS

BAD LOCATION

SINGLE FOUNDER

RAISING TOO LITTLE MONEY

HIRING BAD EMPLOYEES

NOT PUTTING IN ENOUGH EFFORT

BAD PLANNING/ STRUCTURE

WRONG AUDIENCE TARGETING

CHOOSING THE WRONG PLATFORM

POOR INTERNAL MANAGEMENT

WHAT NOBODY'S TELLING YOU

1. The average millionaire has **7 sources** of income.

2. Only **1 in 9** business really survive.

3. **22.5%** of small business fail in the first year.

So stop talking and get to work!

DIDN'T EXIST IN 2007

INSTAGRAM   UBER   SNAPCHAT   BITCOIN   WHATSAPP

IPAID   SLACK   TESLA   ANDROID   AIRBNB

4G   PINTEREST   SPOTIFY   BEATS   BLOCKCHAIN

WHAT IS STOPPING YOU FROM BECOMING THE NEXT STORY

IF YOU CAN'T MAKE MONEY, DO THIS

1) **CHOOSE** A BUSINESS MODEL → Let's say you choose email marketing.

2) **STUDY IT** FOR 30 DAYS → Buy courses and watch Youtube videos.

3) **SELL IT** FOR 30 DAYS → Get on the phone and sell your service.

4) **PERFECT IT** FOR 30 DAYS → Get your clients the best results that you can.

IF YOU FOCUS AND DO IT CORRECTLY, YOU WILL MAKE **$5K- $10K A MONTH.**

What **society** tells you in cool:

- College degree
- $100k salary
- Mercedes
- Bottle service

What is **actually** cool:

- Eating Asian food in Asia
- Unlimited earning potential
- Financial Independence
- Starting a charity

Your family and friends won't understand until you **"make it"**

Keep grinding. They'll realize what you're accomplishing in **due time.**

SETTING GOALS
RICH VS POOR

"I wanna be rich someday..."
- **Some poor guy**

"I plan to earn **X** by **Y** with **Z**"
- **Every rich guy ever**

X - Specific $$ Amount

Y - Specific Date

Z - Exactly How You

   Plan To Earn It.

WANT TO RETIRE AT 65 WITH $1 MILLION?

Here's how much you would have to
Save Each Month if you started at:

25 Years Old: **$415**
30 Years Old: **$599**
35 Years Old: **$877**
40 Years Old: **$1,309**
45 Years Old: **$2,018**
50 Years Old: **$3,288**
55 Years Old: **$5,965**
60 Years Old: **$14,210**

6 CLASSES THAT SHOULD BE MANDATORY IN HIGH SCHOOL

 Money Management

 Mental Health

 Taxes

 Time Management

 Act of Kindness

 Financial Literacy

SNOWBALL EFFECT

The snowball effect is a concept
that is especially **true in business.**

It's the very reason why getting started
is the hardest part of **entrepreneurship.**

Once you have started you gain
momentum and slowly a snowball.

**NOW YOU JUST
NEED TO
START!**

INNOVATE OR DIE

AMAZON VS. **RETAIL**   **AIRBNB** VS. **HOTELS**   **UBER/LYFT** VS. **TAXIS**   **NETFLIX** VS. **CABLE**

IF YOU FAIL TO **INNOVATE**, YOU WILL **CEASE TO EXIST** IN BUSINESS.

DON'T BE THE NEXT KODAK, BLOCKBUSTER, OR **TOYS "R" US.**

Your family and friends won't understand until you **"make it"**

Keep grinding. They'll realize what you're accomplishing in **due time.**

INVESTING BY AGE

UNDER 30

CASH 5%
REAL ESTATE 10%
GOLD 15%
STOCKS 70%

30 TO 50

CASH 5%
REAL ESTATE 10%
GOLD 20%
STOCKS 65%

45 TO 60

CASH 15%
REAL ESTATE 12.5%
GOLD 27%
STOCKS 45%

ABOVE 60

CASH 20%
STOCKS 30%
REAL ESTATE 15%
GOLD 35%

DUMBEST WAYS TO GO BROKE

BUYING THINGS TO
IMPRESS OTHERS

BUYING THINGS THAT
HARM YOUR HEALTH

INVESTING IN THINGS
YOU DON'T UNDERSTAND

GAMBLING & TRYING
TO GET RICH QUICK

BEST INVESTING BOOKS

The Intelligent Investor	**Benjamin Graham**
A Random Walk Down Wall street	**Burton Malkiel**
Rich Dad Poor Dad	**Robert Kiyosaki**
The Warren Buffett Way	**Robert G. Hangstorm**
One Up On Wall Street	**Peter Lynch**
Money: Master The Game	**Tony Robbins**

A LESSON ON SCALING

Example: **Dog walking**

Get paid **$15 for 1 hour.** Do the walking yourself.

Get paid **$15 for 1 hour.** Hire a walker for $10.

While the profit is greater per client, you are limited by your time.

While the profit is less per client, you are not limited by your time.

This is not scalable.

This is scalable.

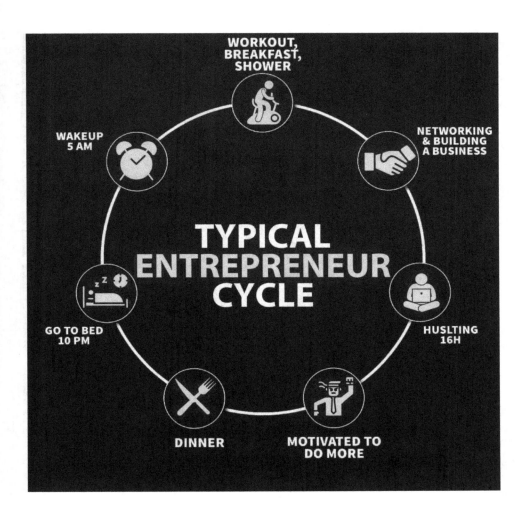

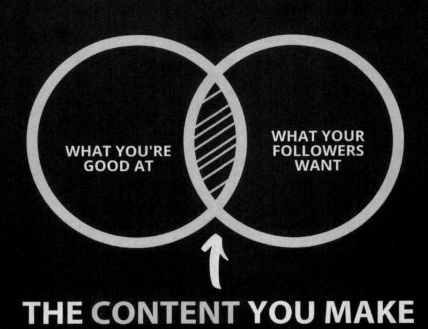

AREAS YOU CAN CUT EXPENSES

CABLE BILL

ELECTRICITY BILL

PHONE BILL

STARBUCKS COFFEE

EATING OUT

SUBSCRIPTION SERVICES

SHOPPING EXPENSES

GROCERIES EXPENSES

NAME BRAND ITEMS

TIPS FROM BILLIONAIRES

**THE BIGGEST RISK IS NOT
TAKING ANY RISKS.**
- MARK ZUCKERBERG

**WHEN SOMETHING IS IMPORTANT
ENOUGH. YOU DO IT EVEN IF THE
ODDS ARE NOT IN YOUR FAVOR.**
- ELON MUSK

**THE THINGS YOU REGRET THE MOST IN
LIFE ARE THE THINGS YOU DIDN'T DO.**
- STEVE JOBS

WORK LIKE HELL

"WORK LIKE HELL,
I MEAN YOU HAVE TO PUT IN
80 TO 100 HOUR WEEKS
EVERY WEEK. THIS IMPROVES
THE ODDS OF SUCCESS.
IF OTHER PEOPLE ARE PUTTING
IN 40 HOUR WORKWEEKS
AND YOU'RE PUTTING IN
100 HOUR WORKWEEKS,
THEN EVEN IF YOU'RE DOING
THE SAME THING YOU KNOW
THAT YOU WILL ACHIEVE IN
4 MONTHS WHAT IT TAKES
THEM A YEAR TO ACHIEVE."

- ELON MUSK

HOW TO DOMINATE SOCIAL MEDIA

1 BE AUTHENTIC: PEOPLE ARE TIRED OF POLISHED LIVES

2 STICK TO YOUR NICHE: DON'T TRY TO PLEASE EVERYONE

3 HIT PUBLISH: DON'T LET PERFECTION PARALYSIS STOP YOU

4 FIND YOUR OWN VOICE: DON'T TRY TO SPEAK LIKE OTHERS

5 BE CONSISTENT: MAKE COMMITMENT TO POST REGULARLY

6 MAKE FRIENDS: INTERACT WITH THE LEADERS IN YOUR INDUSTRY

7 CHOOSE WELL: PICK THE PLATFORMS WHERE YOU IDEAL CLIENTS ARE

8 BE SOCIAL: IT SHOULD BE A 2 WAY CONVERSATION, NOT A MONOLOGUE

9 TEST AND TRACK: CHECK YOUR ANALYTICS TO KNOW WHAT CONTENT WORKS BEST

10 PROVIDE VALUE: MAKE SURE EACH PIECE OF CONTENT SERVES YOUR AUDIENCE

EASIEST WAY TO
DROPSHIP WITH SHOPIFY

CREATE & DESIGN A STORE
WITH SHOPIFY

DOWNLOAD THE OBERLO
APP TO FULFILL ORDERS
THROUGH ALIEXPRESS

IMPORT PRODUCTS FROM
ALIEXPRESS WITH OBERLO TO
YOUR SHOPIFY STORE

HOW TO DO PRODUCT RESEARCH FOR SHOPIFY

1. SEARCH FOR THE PRODUCT YOU PICKED ON ALIEXPRESS

2. WHEN YOU'VE FOUND THE PRODUCT YOU PICKED, FIND IT'S SUPPLIERS AND THEN..⬇

3. CHECK HOW MANY ORDERS, REVIEWS AND STARS THE PRODUCT HAS.

IF IT HAS GOOD REVIEWS/STARS AND HIGH ORDER COUNT.
YOU HAVE FOUND YOUR WINNING PRODUCT!

IF YOU WANT A BETTER LIFE

You have to be willing to pay the
"TRUE COST" of better life.

1. Late nights.

2. Waking up early.

3. Investing money.

4. Dropping bad habits.

5. Learning good habits.

6. Being sore from the gym.

7. Learning new information.

8. Leaving behind old friends.

9. Being turned down & rejected.

7 TIMELESS RULES
ABOUT MONEY

1. Never rely on one source of income.

2. Save at least 10% of your income.

3. Never increase expenses with income.

4. You need to develop a money mindset.

5. Don't go broke trying to impress others.

6. Never stop learning and invest in yourself.

7. Avoid bad debt at all the cost.

Watching Netflix every day after work is easy.

Skipping the gym and eating comfort foods is easy.

Not working on your business and partying is easy.

Spending all your money at the mall is easy.

Gossiping about politics, sports and your old friends is easy.

Easy doesn't pay well.

INVEST IN YOU

01. Watch Educational Shows
02. Learn Stuff Online
03. Stay in Touch with Family
04. Read Books or eBooks
05. Choose Your Friends Wisely
06. Get Rid of Toxic Friends
07. Find a Mentor
08. Start That Business
09. Start a New Hobby
10. Learn a Language
11. Set Goals
12. Plan Your Day and Week
13. Make a Plan for Your Life
14. Practice Gratitude
15. Practice Meditation
16. Exercise
17. Learn More Skills
18. Drink Less Alcohol

19. Don't Worry About Options
20. Eat Healthier
21. Learn to Cook
22. Sleep and Wake Up Earlier
23. Stop Procrastinating
24. Manage Your Time Better
25. Stick to a Routine
26. Travel More.
27. Save Your Money
28. Invest Your Money
29. Spend Money on Experiences
30. Challenge Yourself Daily
31. Visualize Success
32. Forgive Others
33. Stop Trying to Win Approval
34. Take Pride in Your Appearance
35. Love Yourself
36. Listen to Podcasts

What's your excuses today?
Too tired?
Too sore?
Too busy?
Whatever it is, it's a lie.

The real reason why you're not doing it is
because it's not important enough to you.

You have to make your dream an
emergency. You've got to be willing to do
whatever it takes at any time, anywhere.
No matter what.

Once you do that on a daily basis, they you'll
make it a reality.

COMFORT IS A DRUG

Once you get used to it, it becomes addicting.

Give a weak man consistent sex, good food, cheap entertainment and he'll throw his ambitions right out the window.

The comfort zone is where dreams go to die.

65 WAYS YOU CAN MAKE $3000 FROM HOME

01. Executive VA
02. General VA
03. Marketing VA
04. Public Relations
05. Community Manager
06. Social Media Manager
07. Web Designer
08. Flier Services
09. Etsy Seller
10. Graphic Designer
11. Photographer
12. Videographer
13. Music Composer
14. Stock Music Seller
15. Voice Over Actor
16. Scrapbooking
17. Landscape Designer
18. Homeschooler
19. Courthouse Research
20. Errands Service
21. Order Fulfillment
22. Seamstress
23. Baker
24. Car Detailer
25. Chef
26. Bike Messenger
27. Dog Walker
28. Pet Sitting
29. Direct Sales
30. Driver
31. Outbound Sales
32. Event Planner
33. Travel Agent
34. Transcription
35. Podcast Editing
36. Document Convert
37. User Testing
38. Podcasting
39. Blogging
40. Search Evaluator
41. Coaching
42. Online Selling
43. Mystery Shopper
44. Amazon FBA
45. Shopify
46. Sell T-Shirts
47. Affiliate Marketing
48. Home Tutor
49. Online Tutor
50. Music Lessons
51. Online Teacher
52. Magazine Writer
53. Copywriter
54. Author
55. Bookkeeper
56. Proofreader
57. Project Manager
58. Consultant
59. Yoga Instructor
60. Life Coach
61. YouTuber
62. Twitch Streamer
63. Cooking Show
64. Product Reviewer
65. Exercise Instructor

TODAY'S SOCIETY

"How to buy index funds"
13 views

"Stock market basics"
54 views

"Billionaires morning routine"
47,083,203 views

30 WAYS TO MAKE PROGRESS

01. Wake up early	11. Find inspiration	21. Learn skills
02. Read daily	12. Help others	22. Invest
03. Eat well	13. Network	23. Journal
04. Love yourself	14. Save money	24. Meditate
05. Judge less	15. Automate	25. Get a mentor
06. Be yourself	16. Delegate	26. Think big
07. Set goals	17. Track finances	27. Be productive
08. Plan your day	18. Build a brand	28. Do more
09. Positive attitude	19. Fail fast	29. Spend wisely
10. Have purpose	20. Interact	30. Be ambitious

THE MATH BEHIND SIDE HUSTLES

JOSH

Makes $40,000/year

Earns $200/week from his side hustle

First year : $50,400

Fifth year : $252,000

ALEX

Makes $40,000/year

Spends $200/week on going out

First year : $29,600

Fifth year : $148,000

The biggest financial advantage you can give yourself in your 20s is resisting the urge to impress anyone. Live in a small place, drive a modest car, Keep a simple wardrobe, and patiently accumulate assets that will give you freedom for the next 6-7 decades.

EVERY TIME YOU

01. Stay out late
02. Sleep in
03. Party all weekend
04. Miss a workout
05. Overreact
06. Sit on the couch
07. Say you'll start tomorrow
08. Complain
09. Don't give 100%
10. Procrastinate

Your competition is winning.

Remember that.

MONEYTUTORSHIP
@moneytutorship

You gotta step out of your comfort zone,
Be broke for a while. Lose some friends.
Have some sleepless nights. Most people
don't get it through.

A FACT ABOUT MONEY

If you can't manage $1,000 then
you can't manage $10,000.

You don't suddenly learn how to
handle money by amassing more
of it. This is why a lot of lottery
winners lose it all.

Financial literacy is not a side
effect of wealth. Wealth is a side
effect of financial literacy.

College: $40,000
Wedding: $30,000
House: $250,000
Used Car: $10,000

Over $300,000 in debt after your first few years after graduating from College but society will call you a loser if you don't follow this debt trap.

YOU MUST INCREASE YOUR INCOME

Canceling Netflix for $10/month
isn't going to help you.

Making your own coffee to
save $5 isn't going to help you.

Income must be increased!

Cutting back on basic garbage is fine but
don't pretend you're making progress.

Make more money,
spend it however you want.

Watching Netflix every day after work is easy.

Skipping the gym and eating comfort foods is easy.

Not working on your business and partying is easy.

Spending all your money at the mall is easy.

Gossiping about politics, sports and your old friends is easy.

Easy doesn't pay well.

ADVICE TO MY YOUNGER SELF

01. Read more.
02. Write more.
03. Practice public speaking.
04. Value friendship.
05. Memorizing is not learning.
06. Learn to invest.
07. You are not your job.
08. Know when to leave.
09. Find a mentor.
10. Trust your gut.
11. Slove your harder problems.
12. Networking is about giving.

8 INCOME STREAMS

1. Earned Income   - Income from working a job

2. Profit Income   - Income from buying and selling

3. Interest Income - Income from lending money

4. Royalty Income   - Income from others using your idea

5. Dividend Income - Income from owning stocks

6. Rental Income   - income from renting a property

7. Capital gains   - Assets increasing in value

8. Residual Income - When you continue to get paid
                      after the work is done

RULES OF MONEY

01. Pay yourself first.
02. Learn how to invest.
03. Don't be a hater of it.
04. Give every dollar a job.
05. Spend less than you earn.
06. Have a plan and set goals.
07. Don't be a slave of money.
08. If you have it, don't flaunt it.
09. Keep your finances organized.
10. It's a game, learn how it works.
11. Always have an emergency fund.
12. Always make money work for you.
13. Learn how to make money passively.
14. Use it to solve problems in the world.
15. Know how to risk it and leverage it.
16. Don't use credit if you don't have cash.
17. It's not what you make, it's what you keep.

YOU HAVE A DAILY CHOICE

MUSIC

FASTFOOD

SOCIAL MEDIA

SPEND MONEY

OR

OR

OR

OR

PODCAST

SALAD

BOOKS

INVEST MONEY

THE RICH
AND POOR

	RICH		POOR
	7	Sources of income	1
	✖	Watch tv	✔
	✔	Read daily	✖
	✖	Make excises	✔
	✔	Grind daily	✖

12 HABITS THAT DRAIN YOUR WALLET

$5 Coffees

Bottled water

Lottery tickets

Eating out daily

Paid phone apps

Cigarettes

Credit card fees

Unnecessary uber's

Unused subscriptions

Not searching for discounts

Over priced cell phone

Spending money at the bar

THERE ARE TWO
KINDS OF PEOPLE

✔ SLEEP UNTIL NOON	✔ WAKE UP EARLY
✔ SKIP EXCERCISE	✔ GET THEIR EXCERCISE
✔ EAT JUNK FOOD	✔ EAT HEALTHY
✔ LIVE MINDLESSLY	✔ WORK ON NEW SKILLS
✔ WASTE YEARS OF THEIR LIFE	✔ FOCUS ON SELF-GROWTH
✔ BLOW THIER PAYCHECKS	✔ CONTROL THEIR FINANCES
✔ ALWAYS IN THE SAME PLACE	✔ ALWAYS MOVING FORWARD

SKILLS THAT CAN PAY $10,000 PER MONTH

COPYWRITING

CODING

FUNNEL BUILDING

CONTENT CREATION

BUILDING BRANDS

WRITING EMAILS

SOCIAL MEDIA GROWTH

GRAPHIC DESIGN

WHAT ARE YOU DOING WITH YOUR PHONE?

INSTEAD OF...

- ✖ WASTING TIME
- ✖ PLAYING GAMES
- ✖ WATCHING VIDEOS
- ✖ WATCHING MOVIES
- ✖ FOLLOWING PEOPLE
- ✖ OPENING NOTIFICATIONS
- ✖ CONTINUOUS SCROLLING

DO THIS...

- ✔ LEARN INVESTING
- ✔ SELL PRODUCTS
- ✔ MAKE SHOPS
- ✔ CREATE PAGES
- ✔ FLIP ITEMS
- ✔ WATCH COURSES
- ✔ DEVELOP GOOD HABITS

BROKE VS RICH

BROKE

JUMP ON
EVERY TREND

BUY BRANDED
CLOTHES

INVEST IN CARS
& SNEAKERS

PARTY ON THE
WEEKEND

RICH

INVEST IN
THE TREND

CLOTHES AREN'T
IMPORTANT

SPEND MONEY
ON BOOKS
AND COURSES

WORK TOWARDS
THEIR DREAM
DAILY

ADVICE BY 21 SAVAGE

"I stopped wearing jewelry for a couple of reasons.
One is because everybody wears jewelry. I outgrew it;
I'm getting a little wiser and growing so... Another reason
is because the richest people that I've ever met in my life,
they've never had on jewelry."

A LESSON ABOUT MONEY

Society teaches us to look at
money like this: 40 hour a week
for $15 an hour = $600

Imagine looking at money like this:
60 sales x $50 order = $3000

There's a cap on how many
hours/day you can work, but there
is NO CAP on the number of sales
your business can make.

THE BIGGEST MONEY WASTERS

SMOKING

EXPENSIVE CLOTHES

BOTTLED WATER

GAMBLING

JEWELRY

EXPENSIVE CARS

FAST FOOD

BREAK YOUR BAD HABITS

It's supposed to take 21 days before doing
something constantly becomes a habit.

Just think: 21 days without binging, can
become a lifetime.

21 days of going to the gym will make you not
even think twice about going anymore.

21 days of saying "no, thank you" to sugary treats.

21 days of working on your side hustle after your
9-5 to get rid of procrastination once and for all.

All it takes is 21 days of dedication.
why not start now?

HOW TO HAVE MORE TIME

01. Works in blocks.

02. Learn how to say no.

03. Cut down on TV/Netflix.

04. Plan your week in advance.

05. Limit your social media time.

06. Don't be busy just to be busy.

07. Don't do everything... delegate.

08. Unsubscribe from useless emails.

09. Don't be a perfectionist all the time.

10. Do most important tasks in the AM.

11. Be good at planning and organizing.

12. Disable notifications for useless apps.

13. Find tasks to eliminate or auomate.

14. One task to eliminate or automate.

15. Always set reminders on your phone.

16. Write stuff down so you don't forget.

If you're reading this, I DARE YOU to dedicate the next 6 months exclusively to your goals. No annoucments, just fall back & do the work!

YOU NEED TO MAKE

$2,740 PER DAY
FOR 365 DAYS

...to make
$1,000,000
a year.

Here's the blueprint:

Product + Funnel + Paid Ads =

Less Soda, more Water.

Less Alcohol, more Tea.

Less Sugar, more Fruits.

Less Meat, more Vegetables.

Less Driving, more Walking.

Less Anger, more laughter.

Less Worry, more Sleep.

Less Words, more Action.

Business is won by players who focus on the playing field, not by those whose eyes are glued to the scoreboard.

YOUR NEW HABITS FOR 2020

QUITING WITH BAD HABITS

SAVE AND INVEST $500/MONTH

LEARN A NEW SKILL EVERY MONTH

READ 2 BOOKS PER MONTH

WORKOUT AT LEAST 2X A WEEK

I've seen people workout at 4 AM before working two jobs.

I've known introverts who became great communicators when an important relationship needed it.

I've seen people who weren't "ready" suddenly commit to the right person.

People give effort to what's important to them.

"SUCCESS IS MY DUTY, RESPONSIBILITY AND OBLIGATION"

- GRANT CARDONE

IN A FEW MONTHS 97% OF PEOPLE WILL GO BACK TO THE WAY THINGS WERE

- Complaining about their job
- Bad spending habits
- Not preparing for the future

3% WILL COME BACK STRONGER

- Learned new skills
- Started a new business
- Invested in the future

Which group will you be in?

SKILLS ARE HIGHLY RECOMMEND

CODING

MARKETING

FINANCE

INVESTING

SALES

GRAPHIC DESIGN

MONEY IS GOOD

It gives you the capacity to afford to acquire and do many good things.

On the flip side of the coin, it also empowers you to commit sin you could not afford before.

You can have a 9-5 AND have rental properties.

You can have a 9-5 AND have vending machines.

You can have a 9-5 AND invest in the stock market.

You can have a 9-5 AND wholesale real estate.

You can have a 9-5 AND be an entrepreneur!

SUCCESS IS STILL YOUR
DUTY EVEN DURING
A QUARANTINE.

- GRANT CARDONE

BEST BUSINESS
IF YOU'RE BROKE

BUSINESS IDEA	COST
UX DESIGN AGENCY	$10
DIGITAL AGENCY	$10
BOT MARKETING AGENCY	$0
FREELANCE COPYWRITER	$80
FREELANCE APP DEVELOPER	$90
PROFESSIONAL CONSULTANT	$0
GHOST WRITER	$0
EVENT PLANNER	$0
CITY-WIDE TAXI SERVICE	$80
WEDDING PLANNER	$80
PET SITTING	$100

A doctor learns & understands medicine to earn money.

A lawyer learns & understands law to earn money.

A dietitian learns & understands nutrition to earn money.

A chef learns & understands culinary to earn money.

Yet, don't you think it's strange nobody learns & understands money?

THINGS YOU CAN CONTROL

YOUR
ATTITUDE

YOUR
NETWORK

YOUR
HABITS

YOUR
WORK RATE

YOUR
GRATITUDE

YOUR
PHYSIQUE

GIVE YOURSELF 6 MONTHS

6 Months to be consistent at 1 thing.

- Hitting the gym
- Learning a new skill
- Creating/Selling a product
- Growing an audience

If you can stay consistent for 6 months, you're going to see changes in your life.

That feeling is unsurpassed.

RISK

IF YOU DON'T MAKE IT,
IT'S YOUR OWN DAMN "FAULT".

INDUSTRIES THAT MAKE PEOPLE RICH

REAL ESTATE

FINANCE

HEALTH CARE

LOGISTICS

TECHNOLOGY

RETAIL

ENERGY

MEDIA

CONSTRUCTION

I WOKE UP. I HAVE CLOTHES TO WEAR.
I HAVE RUNNING WATER.
I HAVE FOOD TO EAT.
LIFE IS GOOD. I AM THANKFUL.

THIS IS WHY YOU NEED TO BE FINANCIALLY PREPARED

A financial emergency is not a matter of "if" but "when".

Having an adequate emergency fund can get you through times when income is low or nonexistent.

Those who had money set aside for an emergency are better able to weather this current storm.

How much shoud you save? I recommend three to six months worth of living expenses, depending on how many are reliant on your income.

A financial emergency will happen, and we must be prepared.

THE BENEFITS OF AN ONLINE BUSINESS

Global access, 365 days/year, 7 days/week, 24 hours/day.

Improved client service through greater flexibility.

Increased professionalism.

Faster delivery of products.

Less paper waste.

Less expenses = Higher profit margin.

Opportunities to manage your business from anywhere in the world.

IF YOU ARE WORKING ON SOMETHING
EXCITING THAT YOU ARE REALLY
CARE ABOUT YOU DON'T HAVE TO BE
PUSHED. THE VISION PULLS YOU.

BEST BUSINESS
IF YOU'RE BROKE

BUSINESS IDEA	COST
UX DESIGN AGENCY	$10
DIGITAL AGENCY	$10
BOT MARKETING AGENCY	$0
FREELANCE COPYWRITER	$80
FREELANCE APP DEVELOPER	$90
PROFESSIONAL CONSULTANT	$0
GHOST WRITER	$0
EVENT PLANNER	$0
CITY-WIDE TAXI SERVICE	$80
WEDDING PLANNER	$80
PET SITTING	$100

YOU HAVE A
DAILY CHOICE

MUSIC

FASTFOOD

SOCIAL
MEDIA

SPEND
MONEY

OR

OR

OR

OR

PODCAST

SALAD

BOOKS

INVEST
MONEY

If you hang around people that only make you feel good, you are hanging out with fake people.

You can't grow around comfort zone people.

You say it's disrespectful when someone insults you by telling you their honest perspective.

I say it's more disrespectful to lie to someone to make them feel good.

A person telling you the truth is the greatest sign of respect.

When people lie to you, it's either because:

They think you are too weak and emotional to take it or you're too dumb to notice.

ENTREPRENEURSHIP 101

Don't borrow money - Lend it

Don't take a job - Create one

Don't dig for gold - Sell shovels

Don't see a problem - See a solution

Don't buy a fish - Teach people how to fish

HOW TO BUILD YOUR PASSIVE INCOME

YOUR 9-5 INCOME FUELS YOUR SIDE HUSTLE

YOUR SIDE HUSTLE FUELS YOUR INVESTMENTS

YOUR INVESTMENTS REPLACES YOUR 9-5 INCOME

THE MATH BEHIND SIDE HUSTLES

JOSH

Makes $40,000/year

Earns $200/week from his side hustle

First year : $50,400

Fifth year : $252,000

ALEX

Makes $40,000/year

Spends $200/week on going out

First year : $29,600

Fifth year : $148,000

THE POWER OF A
SIDE HUSTLES

$25/week = $1,300/year
$50/week = $2,600/year
$100/week = $5,200/year
$200/week = $10,400/year
$500/week = $26,000/year
$1000/week = $52,000/year

Please keep in mind: The difference between the clever &
the stupid is that the clever guy aims for $25/week working
4h/day and scales it to $1,000/week while reducing the work
to 2h/day which equals $71.43/h of active work while...

...the idiot aims for the $1k/week working 4h/day & quits
because he only hits the $25 & feels like working for $0.89/h
is a joke so he doesn't even think about scaling systematically.

PATH IN 2 DIFFERENT  PERSPECTIVE 👍

Something to avoid,
harmful & negative,
destructive.

COMFORT

Something to fight through
building & forming character
constructive.

GREATNESS

Remember that the road of the lowest resistance never
leads to a beautiful destination in life. See pain as weakness
leaving the body or a challenge given to you by life and fight!

BROKE VS RICH

BROKE

JUMP ON
EVERY TREND

BUY BRANDED
CLOTHES

INVEST IN CARS
& SNEAKERS

PARTY ON THE
WEEKEND

RICH

INVEST IN
THE TREND

CLOTHES AREN'T
IMPORTANT

SPEND MONEY
ON BOOKS
AND COURSES

WORK TOWARDS
THEIR DREAM
DAILY

NEVER BUY A BRAND NEW CAR

YOUR CARS VALUE WILL DECREASE BY 20% TO 30% BY THE END OF THE FIRST YEAR.

INSTEAD, BUY A USED CAR. THAT IS JUST COMING OFF A 2 TO 3 YEARS LEASE.

THESE CARS ARE STILL NEW AND SHINY WITH LOW MILEAGE, BUT THEY COST 30% LESS.

SHOULD YOU SAVE OR INVEST?

 SAVE   ✓ INVEST

MIKE HAS A $1500 EMERGENCY FUND, A STEADY SOURCES OF INCOME AND NO DEBT.

✓ SAVE   INVEST

ANDY HAS A $800 EMERGENCY FUND, AN UNPREDICTABLE INCOME AND $2000 IN DEBT.

✓ SAVE   INVEST

TOM DOESN'T HAVE AN EMERGENCY FUND, DOES NOT HAVE A JOB AND NO DEBT.

IF YOU DON'T HAVE AN EMERGENCY FUND, SAVE.

IF YOU ARE IN DEBT, SAVE.

IF YOU HAVE AN EMERGENCY FUND AND NO DEBT, INVEST.

THERE ARE 252 WORKING DAYS THIS YEAR

IF YOU WORK A 9-5 YOU AREN'T PAID
FOR 2 DAYS OF EVERY WEEK, LIMITING
YOUR ABILITY TO GET WEALTHIER.

YOU SPEND MONEY 100% OF
THE DAYS, BUT YOU ONLY
MAKE MONEY 69% OF THE
DAYS.

IF YOU SPEND MONEY
EVERYDAY, THEN YOU
SHOULD MAKE MONEY EVERYDAY

RULES OF MONEY

01. Pay yourself first.
02. Learn how to invest.
03. Don't be a hater of it.
04. Give every dollar a job.
05. Spend less than you earn.
06. Have a plan and set goals.
07. Don't be a slave of money.
08. If you have it, don't flaunt it.
09. Keep your finances organized.
10. It's a game, learn how it works.
11. Always have an emergency fund.
12. Always make money work for you.
13. Learn how to make money passively.
14. Use it to solve problems in the world.
15. Know how to risk it and leverage it.
16. Don't use credit if you don't have cash.
17. It's not what you make, it's what you keep.

8 SIGNS YOU ARE GOOD WITH MONEY

YOU HAVE A STEADY FLOW OF INCOME

YOU KNOW HOW MUCH YOU SPEND

YOU CAN PAY YOUR BILLS EVERY MONTH

YOU CAN BUY THINGS YOU WANT

YOU HAVE AN EMERGENCY FUND

YOU ARE PLANNING FOR A MAJOR PURCHASE

YOU ARE SAVING MONEY

YOU INVEST TO MAKE MORE MONEY

A $100K SALARY
DOESN'T MEAN ANYTHING

If you're working like a hamster
in a wall street cubicle nonstop.

Money is only 1/3 of the equation.
The rest are location and time freedom.

To be truly rich, you need to work remotely.
as little as possible and make a lot of money.

HOW TO INVEST $1000

25%	25%	25%	25%
FOODS & BEVERAGES	PHARMA & HEALTH CARE	AI & ROBOTICS	IT SOFTWARE & SERVICES

• COCA-COLA	• NOVARTIS	• IBM	• APPLE
• PEPSICO	• PFIZER	• NVIDIA	• GOOGLE
• MCDONALDS	• ABBVIE	• HISILICON	• MICROSOFT
• STARBUCKS	• J&J	• INTEL	• FACEBOOK
• NESCAFE	• SANOFI	• ALIBABA	• AMAZON

F*CK PEOPLE

BUY THE RED CAR.
People will say you should've got blue.

START A BUSINESS.
People will say you should've got a job.

GET MARRIED.
People will say you picked the wrong partner.

LEARN A TRADE.
People will say you should've went to college.

Everyone has a opinion about everything.
You'll go crazy trying to please everyone.
Don't even try.

Listen, Smile, Agree and then do whatever
the f*ck you were gonna do anyway.

BEGINNER MISTAKES
AS AN ENTREPRENEUR

Mistake #1	No plan
Mistake #2	Spending too much money first
Mistake #3	Expecting fast results for no effort
Mistake #4	Hiring too soon
Mistake #5	Not surveying potential clients
Mistake #6	Copying others
Mistake #7	Not passionate about your business
Mistake #8	Doing it alone
Mistake #9	Thinking busy is productive
Mistake #10	Not starting today

EN-TRE-PRE-NEUR:

KANYE WEST IN
HIS 20'S

KANYE WEST TIME
MAGAZINE COVER 2015

A PERSON WHO'S UP LATE WORKING 80 HOURS OR
MORE A WEEK FOR THEMSELVES, TO AVOID
WORKING 40 HOUR A WEEK FOR SOMEONE ELSE.

THE RICH
AND POOR

	RICH		POOR
	7	Sources of income	**1**
	✖	Watch tv	✔
	✔	Read daily	✖
	✖	Make excises	✔
	✔	Grind daily	✖

6 MENTAL TRICKS MILLIONAIRES USE

1. Realize there's no shortage of money

2. Think of making money as a game

3. Set their expectations high

4. Block out fear

5. See money as a friend

6. Feel they deserve to be rich

6 WAYS TO
SPARK IDEAS

**SPEAK TO
STRANGERS**

**GO FOR A
WALK**

**WRITE DOWN
DREAMS/IDEAS**

**LISTEN TO
MUSIC**

**EXPLORE NEW PLACES
AND ENVIRONMENTS**

**EMBRACE ALONE
TIME, LET YOUR
MIND WONDER**

RICHEST PEOPLE ON THE EARTH

1.
Jeff Bezos
Amazon(Usa)
$184.2B

2.
Bill Gates
Microsoft(Usa)
$113.5B

3.
Bernard Arnault
LVMH(France)
$112.8B

4.
Mark Zuckerberg
Facebook(Usa)
$88.3B

5.
Mukesh Ambani
Reliance(India)
$75.1B

6.
Larry Elison
Oracle(Usa)
$72.3B

7.
Elon Musk
SpaceX(Usa)
$72.2B

8.
Warren Buffett
B. Hathway(Usa)
$72.2B

9.
Steve Ballmer
Microsoft(Usa)
$71.8B

10.
Larry Page
Google(Usa)
$69.4 B

INVEST IN YOU

01. Watch Educational Shows
02. Learn Stuff Online
03. Stay in Touch with Family
04. Read Books or eBooks
05. Choose Your Friends Wisely
06. Get Rid of Toxic Friends
07. Find a Mentor
08. Start That Business
09. Start a New Hobby
10. Learn a Language
11. Set Goals
12. Plan Your Day and Week
13. Make a Plan for Your Life
14. Practice Gratitude
15. Practice Meditation
16. Exercise
17. Learn More Skills
18. Drink Less Alcohol
19. Don't Worry About Options
20. Eat Healthier
21. Learn to Cook
22. Sleep and Wake Up Earlier
23. Stop Procrastinating
24. Manage Your Time Better
25. Stick to a Routine
26. Travel More.
27. Save Your Money
28. Invest Your Money
29. Spend Money on Experiences
30. Challenge Yourself Daily
31. Visualize Success
32. Forgive Others
33. Stop Trying to Win Approval
34. Take Pride in Your Appearance
35. Love Yourself
36. Listen to Podcasts

THE 4 AREAS OF FOCUS
WHERE TO LOOK FOR PLANNING AND IDEAS GENERATION

INNOVATION

TRENDS
THE FUTURE

NEW INSIGHTS

IMMEDIATE
OPPORTUNITY

YOUR BRAND

WHAT MOTIVATES
US

CUSTOMERS
WHAT MOTIVATES
THEM

UNDIFFERENTIATION

COMPETITORS
THE PAST

WHAT CAN WE
LEARN?

What's your excuses today?
Too tired?
Too sore?
Too busy?
Whatever it is, it's a lie.

The real reason why you're not doing it is
because it's not important enough to you.

You have to make your dream an
emergency. You've got to be willing to do
whatever it takes at any time, anywhere.
No matter what.

Once you do that on a daily basis, they you'll
make it a reality.

YOUR REAL
COMPETITION

Your competition is:

1) The knowledge you neglect to learn.

2) Your lack of discipline.

3) Your procrastination.

4) Your distractions.

5) Your bad habits.

6) Your self-doubt.

7) Your ego.

Compete against that.

THERE ARE 252 WORKING
DAYS THIS YEAR

If you **work a 9-5** you aren't paid for 2 days of every week, limiting your ability to get wealthier.

You spend money **100%** of the days, but you only make money **69%** of the days.

If you **spend** money everyday, then you should **make** money everyday.

HOW TO HAVE
MORE MONEY

INCREASE INCOME

- Start a side hustle.
- Get a better paying job.
- Invest in an index fund.
- Invest in real estate.
- Buy stocks.

DECREASE EXPENSES

- Cancel unused subscriptions.
- Use coupon codes/cashback apps.
- Use the 7-day rule when shopping.
- Stop being materialistic.
- Create a budget & stick to it.

THINGS YOU CAN CONTROL

YOUR
ATTITUDE

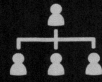

YOUR
NETWORK

YOUR
HABITS

YOUR
WORK RATE

YOUR
GRATITUDE

YOUR
PHYSIQUE

6 RULES TO WIN IN LIFE

1.HAVE A **VISION** FOR YOURSELF

2.COMPARE YOURSELF TO THE **OLD YOU**

3.GROWTH OUTSIDE THE **COMFORT ZONE**

4.READING BOOKS IS AN **ADVANTAGE**

5.STAY **HUMBLE**

6.NEVER QUIT **THE GAME**

HABITS TO STOP RIGHT NOW

1.Living for the weekend
Work on your goals so you can build a life you don't need a vacation from.

2.Running out of money every month
It's time to start watching where every dollar goes and build more discipline for your financial goals.

3.Worrying what other people think
Stop being a prisoner to other people's opinions and letting that effect your life.

4.Not working on your goals after work
Being "too tired" after work is not an excuse. Don't just build someone else's dream at work, take action on your own.

NEXT LEVEL
PASSIVE INCOME

RENT AN APARTMENT FOR $600 A MONTH

RENT OUT YOUR RENTED APARTMENT ON AIRBNB FOR $1000 A MONTH

Fix your body:
Exercise, water, stretch, sun, relax.

 Fix your finances:
Learn, save, invest, create value, sell.

 Fix your mind:
Meditate, read, write, be mindful, gratitude.

 Fix your relationships:
Trust, give, integrity, be honest, respect.

4 WAYS TO GO BROKE

1. ADDICTIONS

2. NO DREAMS & GOALS

3. TOXIC REALTIONSHIPS

4. NO DISCIPLINE

YOU'VE GOT 2 CHOICES IN LIFE:

CHOICE 1:
STEP INTO THE STREAM OF SOMEONE ELSE'S MOMENTUM, WORK FOR THEM 40 YEARS.

CHOICE 2:
CREATE YOUR OWN MOMENTUM, LET OTHERS WORK FOR YOU.

YOU MUST INCREASE YOUR INCOME

Canceling Netflix for $10/month
isn't going to help you.

Making your own coffee to
save $5 isn't going to help you.

Income must be increased!

Cutting back on basic garbage is fine but
don't pretend you're making progress.

Make more money,
spend it however you want.

THIS IS WHY YOU NEED TO BE FINANCIALLY PREPARED

A financial emergency is not a matter of "if" but "when".

Having an adequate emergency fund can get you through times when income is low or nonexistent.

Those who had money set aside for an emergency are better able to weather this current storm.

How much shoud you save? I recommend three to six months worth of living expenses, depending on how many are reliant on your income.

A financial emergency will happen,
<u>and we must be prepared.</u>